I am a Grizzly Bear

Karen Durrie

www.av2books.com

Go to **www.av2books.com**, and enter this book's unique code.

BOOK CODE

P932212

AV² by Weigl brings you media enhanced books that support active learning.

AV² provides enriched content that supplements and complements this book. Weigl's AV² books strive to create inspired learning and engage young minds in a total learning experience.

Your AV² Media Enhanced books come alive with...

 Audio
Listen to sections of the book read aloud.

 Video
Watch informative video clips.

 Embedded Weblinks
Gain additional information for research.

 Try This!
Complete activities and hands-on experiments.

 Key Words
Study vocabulary, and complete a matching word activity.

 Quizzes
Test your knowledge.

 Slide Show
View images and captions, and prepare a presentation.

...and much, much more!

Published by AV² by Weigl
350 5th Avenue, 59th Floor New York, NY 10118
Website: www.av2books.com www.weigl.com

Library of Congress Cataloging-in-Publication Data

Durrie, Karen.
I am a grizzly bear / Karen Durrie. -- 1st ed.
    p. cm. -- (I am)
ISBN 978-1-61913-225-2 (hardcover : alk. paper) -- ISBN 978-1-61913-226-9 (softcover : alk. paper)
1. Grizzly bear--Juvenile literature. I. Title.
QL737.C27D687 2013
599.784--dc23

                        2011042382

Printed in the United States of America in North Mankato, Minnesota
1 2 3 4 5 6 7 8 9 0 16 15 14 13 12

012012
WEP060112

Project Coordinator: Karen Durrie Art Director: Terry Paulhus

Weigl acknowledges Getty Images as the primary image supplier for this title.

I am a Grizzly Bear

In this book, I will teach you about

- **myself**

- **my food**

- **my home**

- **my family**

and much more!

3

I am a grizzly bear.

I am born
when my mother
is sleeping.

6

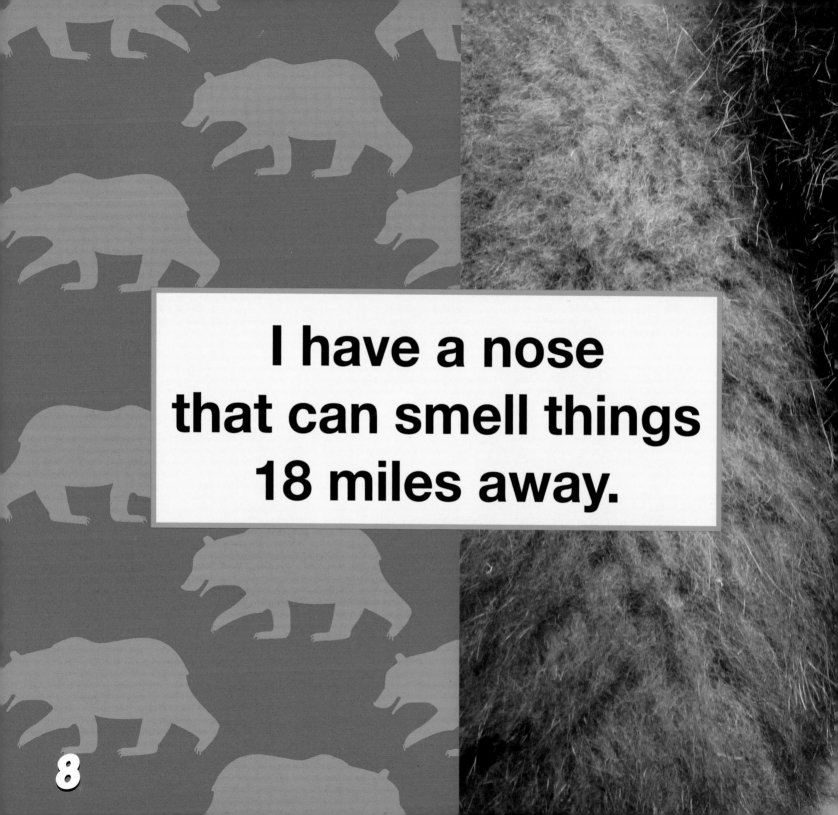

I have a nose
that can smell things
18 miles away.

8

9

I rub my body on trees
to mark where I live.

10

I weigh as much as six adult people.

13

I can run faster than a horse.

I sleep for up to eight months in winter.

17

I can eat 90 pounds of food in one day.

I make my home
in mountain forests
and river valleys.

I am a grizzly bear.

21

GRIZZLY BEAR FACTS

These pages provide detailed information that expands on the interesting facts found in the book. They are intended to be used by adults as a learning support to help young readers round out their knowledge of each amazing animal featured in the I Am series.

Pages 4–5

I am a grizzly bear. The grizzly bear is a type of brown bear that gets its name from the silver, or grizzled, tips of its fur. Grizzly bear coats range from blond to black. Grizzlies live in Alaska, Montana, Idaho, Wyoming, Washington, and the country of Canada.

Pages 6–7

Grizzly bears are born when their mother is sleeping. Cubs are born during the mother's winter sleep. They are usually born in twos, but litters range from one to four. Cubs are born blind but manage to find their mother's milk. When the mother wakes up in spring, her cubs are big enough to leave the den and explore.

Pages 8–9

Grizzly bears have a nose that can smell things 18 miles (29 kilometers) away. The grizzly's sense of smell is one of the keenest in the world, thousands of times stronger than a human's. Scientists have discovered that grizzly bears can detect the smell of people who have been in an area within the last 14 hours.

Pages 10–11

Grizzly bears rub their bodies on logs and trees to mark where they live. Grizzlies mark their territory by biting, scratching, and rubbing tree trunks. Their scent warns other bears that the area is occupied.

Pages 12–13

Grizzly bears weigh as much as six adult people.

The average weight of a male grizzly is about 550 pounds (250 kg). Female grizzlies weigh about 350 pounds (159 kg). Bears living in northern coastal areas can weigh more than 1,000 pounds (454 kg), and reach a height of 7 feet (2.13 meters) tall when standing upright.

Pages 14–15

Grizzly bears can run faster than a horse. Grizzlies can

reach speeds of 35 miles (56 km) per hour. That is more than twice as fast as most people can run. They can outrun horses, but only for short distances. Grizzlies do not have the endurance to run for long periods of time.

Pages 16–17

Grizzly bears sleep for up to eight months in winter.

Grizzly bears go into their dens and hibernate during winter. They do this because there is little food available during winter. They live off the reserves of fat they have stored in their bodies after eating all summer.

Pages 18–19

Grizzly bears can eat 90 pounds (41 kg) of food in

one day. Grizzlies will eat almost anything. Their diet includes roots, berries, insects, fish, rodents, and large animals such as deer. Grizzlies can eat more than 200,000 berries in one day. In late summer, they will eat constantly to get ready for their winter sleep.

Pages 20–21

Grizzly bears live in mountain forests and river

valleys. Grizzly bears are a threatened species. They have lost 98 percent of their habitat due to human activity. There are only about 1,200 grizzlies in the lower 48 states. Their populations in Alaska and Canada are much higher, with 30,000 in Alaska, and 26,000 in Canada.

WORD LIST

Research has shown that as much as 65 percent of all written material published in English is made up of 300 words. These 300 words cannot be taught using pictures or learned by sounding them out. They must be recognized by sight. This book contains 36 common sight words to help young readers improve their reading fluency and comprehension. This book also teaches young readers several important content words, such as proper nouns. These words are paired with pictures to aid in learning and improve understanding.

Page	Sight Words First Appearance	Page	Content Words First Appearance
4	a, am, I	4	bear, grizzly
6	is, mother, my, when	8	nose
8	away, can, have, miles, that, things	10	body, mark
10	live, my, on, to, trees, where	12	adult, six
12	as, much, people	14	horse
14	run, than	16	eight, months, winter
16	for, in, up	18	pounds
18	day, eat, food, of, one,	20	forests, valleys
20	home, make, mountain, river